The Ultimate Guide to Perfect Weddings:

Planning Your Dream Day with Ease and Elegance

By

Virginia E. Riddle

TABLE OF CONTENT

INTRODUCTION:

Welcome to "The Ultimate Guide to Perfect Weddings" your comprehensive companion on the exciting journey of planning and executing a wedding that will be remembered for a lifetime. This book is designed to be your trusted resource, offering a wealth of knowledge, insights, and practical advice to help you confidently and seamlessly manage the intricate world of wedding planning.

A wedding is a celebration of love, a testament to the unique bond between two people, and a declaration of a commitment that will shape your life.

It's a day of dreams and hopes, where your love story takes center stage and is shared with those closest to you.

It's a day filled with joy, emotion, and the promise of a beautiful future.

But, as any couple who has embarked on planning a wedding will tell you, the path to that perfect day is often filled with challenges, questions, and countless decisions from choosing the right venue and designing the perfect invitations to finding the dress that makes you feel like a dream, every step carries unique considerations. That's where this book comes in.

"The Ultimate Guide to Perfect Weddings" is your roadmap to wedding planning success.

Whether you're in the early stages of envisioning your dream wedding or deeply engaged in the finer details, we're here to provide you with the guidance and inspiration you need. We'll help you create a wedding that reflects your personalities and shared love story, ensuring that every element, from the ceremony to the reception, truly reflects who you are as a couple.

Inside these pages, you'll find a treasure trove of advice on budgeting, selecting your dream team of vendors, crafting a beautiful ceremony, and designing a reception that captivates your guests. We'll also delve into the intricate details of attire, catering, entertainment, flowers, and much more.

This book will be your constant companion from the beginning of your planning journey to post-wedding bliss.

We understand that every wedding is unique, just like every love story. This guide provides you with the knowledge and tools to adapt to your specific vision while staying true to the timeless principles of a perfect wedding. We'll offer inspiration from traditions, modern trends, and the limitless possibilities that lie in between.

Your wedding is an opportunity to create a cherished memory that you, your partner, and your loved ones will carry in your hearts for years to come. "

The Ultimate Guide to Perfect Weddings" is your trusted confidant on this transformative journey, and we can't wait to be a part of your incredible story.

So, let's embark on this adventure together and start planning the perfect wedding that reflects your unique love and story. Your journey to "I do" begins here.

CHAPTER 1

Getting Started:

A wedding symbolizes love, a day when dreams take shape and promises are made. Yet, orchestrating this extraordinary event can be a daunting task. Getting started on your wedding planning adventure requires meticulous planning, clear financial goals, and a well-structured timeline. In this book, we'll guide you through these essential first steps to create the wedding of your dreams.

1. Define Your Vision:

Your wedding is a canvas, and your love story is a masterpiece.

Every great wedding begins with a vision. This is where you and your partner come together to imagine your perfect day. Sit down and have an open and honest discussion about what you both envision. Consider the atmosphere, is it a grand, formal occasion or an intimate, rustic gathering? Do you see yourselves exchanging vows on a beach, in a garden, or under the twinkling lights of a ballroom? What emotions do you want to evoke on your special day?

Clearly defining your vision lays the groundwork for your wedding planning journey. This vision will influence all your decisions, from the venue and decor to the attire and overall theme.

Explore your ideas, collect inspiration, and create a shared vision board. This visual representation of your ideas will help you stay focused as you bring your dream to life.

2. Set a Budget:

Financial clarity ensures a memorable day without a financial hangover.

With your vision in place, it's time to address the practical side of wedding planning: setting a budget Your budget is your roadmap, guiding your choices and ensuring financial peace of mind. Begin by taking a candid look at your financial situation. Discuss your budget openly with your partner and any contributing family members.

Set a realistic budget that accounts for your overall expenses.

Research typical wedding costs in your area and style, and allocate your budget to various categories, such as the venue, catering, attire, decor, and entertainment. Remember that some types require more substantial investments, so prioritize according to your vision. Remember to include a contingency fund for unforeseen expenses.

3. Create a Wedding Planning Timeline:

A well-structured timeline is your ally on this incredible journey.

Now that your vision and budget are in place, creating a wedding planning timeline is time.

This timeline will help you stay organized, ensure nothing falls through the cracks, and manage your time efficiently.

Consider the following steps for crafting a comprehensive planning schedule:

12–18 Months Before the Wedding:

Set the wedding date.

Draft a preliminary guest list.

Choose your wedding party.

Research and book your key vendors, including the venue, photographer, and caterer.

9–12 Months Before:

Begin shopping for your wedding attire.

Send out save-the-date cards.

Finalize vendor bookings.

6–9 Months Before:

Plan the ceremony and reception details.

Create a wedding registry.

Make honeymoon arrangements.

4-6 Months Before:

Order wedding invitations and stationery.

Plan pre-wedding celebrations.

Finalize hair and makeup plans.

2-4 Months Before:

Collect RSVPs and create seating arrangements.

Double-check details with all vendors.

Attend your final dress fitting.

1-2 Months Before:

Make final payments to vendors.

Prepare for the wedding day and honeymoon.

The Week of the Wedding:

Ensure all legal documents are in order.

Assemble welcome bags and wedding favors.

Rehearse speeches and toasts.

The Day Before:

Attend the wedding rehearsal and enjoy the rehearsal dinner.

The Wedding Day:

Get ready, celebrate your love, and embrace every moment.

Remember that this timeline is adaptable and can be tailored to suit your specific wedding date and circumstances.

Keep communication open with your partner and your wedding party throughout the planning process. This journey should be a joyful one, a reflection of your unique love story. By defining your vision, setting a budget, and creating a wedding planning timeline, you've taken the first steps toward making your dream day a beautiful reality.

CHAPTER 2

Building Your Dream Team:

Your wedding day is one of the most significant milestones in your life, and to ensure it's a resounding success, you'll need an exceptional team of professionals to bring your vision to life. From the planner who orchestrates the grand affair to the vendors who make the details sparkle, assembling your dream team is a crucial step in wedding planning. In this book, we'll guide you through selecting the right wedding planner, the perfect venue, and the ideal vendors.

1. Choosing the Right Wedding Planner:

Your wedding planner is the conductor of your wedding symphony, ensuring every note is perfectly harmonized.

A skilled wedding planner is a valuable asset to your dream team. They'll help you navigate the intricate world of wedding planning, keeping you organized, on track, and within budget. **Here's how to choose the perfect planner:**

Research and Interviews:

Start by researching potential wedding planners in your area or your wedding destination. Look for those with a portfolio that aligns with your vision. Narrow down your options to a shortlist of planners to interview.

Consultations:

Schedule consultations with your shortlisted planners. During these meetings, discuss your vision, budget, and expectations. Pay attention to their ability to understand your vision and their experience in executing similar weddings.

References and Reviews:

Ask for references and check online reviews. Talking to past clients will give you valuable insights into their work ethic and whether they can deliver on what they promise.

Budget Alignment:

Ensure that the planner's fees align with your budget. A good planner should provide a clear breakdown of their fees and services. Make sure there are no hidden costs.

Personality Match:

Since your wedding planner will work closely with you, your personality must fit well. You should feel comfortable and confident in your planner's abilities.

2. Selecting the Perfect Venue:

Your wedding venue sets the stage; it's where your dream unfolds.

Choosing the right venue is one of the most significant decisions you'll make during your wedding planning journey. It affects the atmosphere, the guest experience, and the overall aesthetics of your day.

Here's how to find the perfect venue:

Consider your vision:

Your venue should align with the vision you've set for your wedding. A ballroom may be ideal if you envision an elegant, formal affair. A garden or barn venue might be the perfect choice for a rustic outdoor celebration.

Location and Accessibility:

Consider the location of the venue and its accessibility for your guests. Consider accommodations and transportation options if you're planning a destination wedding.

Size and capacity:

The venue's size should comfortably accommodate your guest count. Be sure to consider both your ceremony and reception spaces.

Aesthetic Appeal:

Pay attention to the venue's decor, architecture, and style. It should complement your wedding theme and design.

Services and Amenities:

Inquire about the services and amenities offered by the venue, such as catering, setup, and event coordination. This can simplify your planning process.

3. Finding Your Ideal Vendors:

Vendors bring the magic:

They're the artists who craft the details of your dream.

Your choice of vendors, including photographers, caterers, florists, and entertainment, significantly brings your wedding vision to life.

To find the ideal vendors:

Research and Recommendations:

Research vendors in your area and ask for recommendations from your planner, friends, or family. Consider their portfolios and testimonials.

Meet and interview:

Arrange meetings with potential vendors to discuss your vision and requirements. Ask about their experience and the services they offer.

Budget Alignment:

Ensure that their fees fit within your budget. Be transparent about your financial limits.

Contracts and Agreements:

Before finalizing with any vendor, carefully review their contracts. Ensure they include all necessary details, such as services, costs, and deadlines.

References:

Feel free to ask for references and contact previous clients to gain insights into their work ethics and reliability.

Your dream team will turn your vision into a stunning reality. By carefully choosing the right wedding planner, selecting the perfect venue, and finding your ideal vendors, you're well on your way to crafting a wedding day that reflects your love story and makes your dreams come true.

With the right team by your side, your wedding day will surely be nothing short of magical.

CHAPTER 3

Designing Your Day:

Your wedding day is a canvas on which you paint your love story, and ensuring every detail reflects your vision is essential. Designing your wedding involves:

- Choosing themes and styles
- Selecting color schemes and decor.
- Creating the perfect invitations and stationery

This book will explore these aspects of crafting your dream wedding.

1. Wedding Themes and Styles:
Your wedding theme sets the tone, and your style adds a personal touch.

Your wedding theme is the foundation of your design, and it will influence many of your choices, from decor to attire. Consider the following steps when defining your theme and style:

Themes:

Themes can be as diverse as your love story. Whether you're leaning towards a rustic, vintage, modern, or beach wedding, your theme should reflect your personality as a couple. Think about what style resonates most with both of you.

Personalization:

Make it personal by adding elements from your story as a couple.

These could be family traditions, shared hobbies, or significant moments from your relationship.

Consistency:

Ensure that your theme and style are consistent throughout your wedding.

Every aspect should reflect your chosen theme, from the invitations to the ceremony and reception decor.

2. Color Schemes and Décor:

Colors bring your vision to life, while decor adds the finishing touches.

Color is a powerful element in wedding design, and your chosen color scheme will set the tone for your celebration. Follow these steps to select the perfect colors and decor:

Color Palette:

Begin by choosing a color palette that complements your theme and season.

Whether you prefer soft pastels, vibrant jewel tones, or elegant neutrals, your palette will be incorporated into your decor, attire, and more.

Decor Elements:

Think about the decorative elements that will enhance your theme. This could be centerpieces, table linens, lighting, or arches. Your decor should align with your theme and color scheme to create a cohesive atmosphere.

DIY or professional decor:

Consider whether you want to create some decor elements yourself or hire professionals.

DIY decor adds a personal touch, but professionals can execute intricate designs with precision.

Floral Arrangements:

Flowers are an integral part of wedding decor. Select blooms that align with your color scheme and theme. Work closely with your florist to choose the perfect arrangements.

3. Invitations and stationery:

Your invitations are the first glimpse of your wedding style.

Invitations and stationery set the stage for your wedding. They're the first impression your guests have of your big day. Follow these steps to create the perfect invitations and stationery:

Design and Style:

Your invitations should reflect your theme and style. Choose a design that aligns with your vision, whether classic, modern, or whimsical.

Color and Typography:

Select colors and typography that match your color scheme and theme. Be consistent with these choices across all your stationery, from save-the-date cards to ceremony programs.

Details:

Ensure your invitations include all the essential details, such as the date, time, location, and RSVP information. Be clear and concise in your wording.

Personalization:

Add a personal touch by including elements from your love story, such as engagement photos or a custom monogram.

Matching Stationery:

Create matching stationery for the wedding, including place cards, menus, and thank-you cards. Consistency in design attire makes your day beautiful.

Designing your wedding day is an opportunity to express your love story and personality.

By carefully choosing themes and styles, selecting suitable color schemes and decor, and creating stunning invitations and stationery, your wedding will be a beautiful reflection of your unique journey as a couple. Each detail contributes to the masterpiece that is your wedding day.

CHAPTER 4

The Dress and Attire:

Your wedding attire is not just clothing; it's a statement of your love story. It's an expression of your style and an embodiment of your vision. From finding the perfect wedding dress to coordinating bridesmaid's and groomsmen's attire and selecting accessories and the groom's ensemble, your wedding day attire plays a pivotal role in creating a memorable and visually stunning event. In this book, we'll delve into these aspects of wedding attire.

1. Finding the Perfect Wedding Dress:

Your wedding dress symbolizes your love and is an extension of your personality.

Finding the perfect wedding dress is one of the most exciting and sentimental aspects of wedding planning. Here's how to navigate this essential step:

Start Early:

Begin your search for the wedding dress well in advance. Wedding dress shopping typically starts 9–12 months before the wedding to ensure you have enough time for fittings and alterations.

Research and Inspiration:

Research wedding dress styles and gather inspiration from bridal magazines, websites, and social media. Create a mood board to help you pinpoint your preferred style and design.

Bridal Boutiques:

Schedule appointments at bridal boutiques with a range of dress styles.

Try on different silhouettes, necklines, and fabrics to determine what suits you best.

Budget Considerations:

Be clear about your budget when shopping for a wedding dress. Communicate your price range to the bridal boutique consultants to ensure you stay within budget.

Personal Touch:

Consider personalizing your dress with custom alterations, such as embroidery, lace, or other unique details that hold personal significance.

2. Bridesmaids and Groomsmen Attire:

The attire of your bridal party should complement your vision and theme.

Choosing bridesmaids and groomsmen's attire is an essential part of wedding planning, as it contributes to the overall aesthetics of your celebration.

Follow these steps to coordinate their outfits:

Theme and Style:

Ensure your bridal party's attire aligns with your wedding theme and style. Whether you want a classic, modern, or bohemian look, your bridal party dress should reflect your vision.

Color Harmony:

Select colors for bridesmaids' dresses and groomsmen's suits or tuxedos that complement your wedding color scheme. The attire should be cohesive with the overall wedding design.

Coordination:

Coordinate the attire of bridesmaids and groomsmen so they complement each other; this could involve matching colors, styles, or accessories.

Comfort and Personalization:

Keep the comfort of your bridal party in mind. You can allow some individuality in their attire while maintaining a cohesive look. For example, bridesmaids could wear dresses in different styles within the same color palette.

3. Accessories and Groom's Attire:

Accessories and the groom's attire are the finishing touches that complete your wedding look.

Accessories and the groom's attire are the final elements to consider when designing your wedding day attire.

Accessories:

Accessories, such as veils, headpieces, jewelry, and shoes, can enhance your overall look. Choose accessories that complement your dress and add a personal touch. Remember essentials like garters and undergarments.

Groom's Attire:

The groom's attire should reflect your wedding style and his personality. Consider options such as traditional tuxedos, suits, or more casual attire, depending on the formality of your wedding.

Ensure the groom's attire matches the theme and color scheme.

Personal Details:

Consider incorporating personal elements into your attire, such as a family heirloom, sentimental jewelry, or custom monogram.

Your wedding attire and your bridal party's attire set the stage for the most important day of your life. By carefully selecting the perfect wedding dress, coordinating bridesmaids and groomsmen's attire, and choosing accessories and the groom's ensemble, you're well on your way to creating a stunning visual tapestry that celebrates your unique love story. These decisions are about more than just clothing; they're about crafting a vision and making a statement about your love and commitment.

CHAPTER 5

Ceremony and Reception Planning:

The ceremony and reception are the heart and soul of your wedding day. It's where you make lasting promises, celebrate your love, and create cherished memories. From selecting the perfect ceremony location to planning a reception that resonates with your vision and choosing the right officiant and ceremony script, this guide explores the vital elements of ceremony and reception planning.

1. Selecting the Ceremony Location:

The ceremony location sets the stage for your vows and the beginning of your journey together.

Choosing the right ceremony location is a significant decision in your wedding planning. Follow these steps to find the ideal setting:

Meaningful Locations:

Consider meaningful places, such as a family church, a beach where you had your first date or a picturesque garden that resonates with your love story.

Venue and weather:

Think about the venue's size and suitability. Consider the season and climate to ensure guest comfort if you opt for an indoor or outdoor ceremony.

Decor and theme:

Ensure that the location aligns with your wedding decor and theme.

The ceremony location sets the visual tone for your wedding, so it should complement your chosen style.

Logistics:

Consider logistics, including accessibility, permits, and any necessary accommodations for guests with special needs.

2. Planning the reception:

The reception celebrates your love and is a feast for the senses.

Planning the reception is about creating an unforgettable experience for your guests.

Here's how to go about it:

Venue Selection:

Choose a reception venue that aligns with your vision and accommodates your guest count.

Consider factors like location, decor, and amenities.

Design and decor:

Work on the design and decor of your reception space. Consider table settings, centerpieces, lighting, and overall aesthetics. Ensure that the decor resonates with your theme and color scheme.

Menu and Catering:

Plan a menu that delights your guests. Collaborate with a caterer to create a meal that aligns with your vision and caters to various dietary preferences.

Entertainment:

Select entertainment options that fit your style, whether a live band, DJ, or cultural performance. Make sure there's a dance floor for guests to celebrate.

Timeline and Flow:

Create a detailed reception timeline to ensure that everything runs smoothly. Include crucial moments like the first dance, toasts, and cake-cutting.

Favors and Keepsakes:

Consider wedding favors and keepsakes for your guests. These could be personalized items or meaningful tokens that reflect your relationship.

3. Officiants and Ceremony Scripts:

Your officiant and ceremony script breathe life into your vows and promises.

The ceremony is the core of your wedding day, and selecting the right officiant and crafting a heartfelt ceremony script are vital components.

Officiant Selection:

Choose an officiant who resonates with your beliefs and values. Whether it's a religious leader, a family member, or a friend, ensure they understand your vision for the ceremony.

Ceremony Script:

Collaborate with your officiant to create a ceremony script that reflects your relationship. Personalize the script with your love story, readings, and vows that hold personal meaning.

Legal Requirements:

Ensure that the ceremony fulfils all legal requirements in your jurisdiction; this may involve obtaining a marriage license, meeting residency requirements, and other legalities.

Rehearsal:

Plan a wedding rehearsal to ensure that the ceremony flows smoothly; this is an opportunity for everyone involved, including the bridal party and officiant, to practice their roles.

The ceremony and reception are the focal points of your wedding day, and careful planning ensures that they reflect your unique love story. By selecting the perfect ceremony location, planning a reception that resonates with your vision, and choosing the right officiant and ceremony script, you'll create an unforgettable celebration that your guests will cherish for years. These decisions are more than just logistics; they're about creating a meaningful and memorable experience that celebrates your love.

CHAPTER 6

Creating Your Registry and Managing: Gifts:

Your wedding registry is not just a wish list; it reflects your new life together. It's an opportunity to express your style, furnish your home, and prepare for the future. Building a wedding registry, understanding gift etiquette, and sending heartfelt thank-you cards are all part of the journey. This guide will explore these aspects of creating your registry and managing wedding gifts.

1. Building Your Wedding Registry:

Your registry is a canvas for your future, a collection of items that tell your unique story.

Building your wedding registry is an exciting part of the wedding planning process. Here's how to create a registry that suits your needs:

Start Early:

Build your registry several months before the wedding; this gives your guests plenty of time to select gifts they know you'll love.

Assess Your Needs:

Think about what items you need as a couple. Consider essentials for your home, such as kitchen appliances, bedding, and furniture. Remember to include things that align with your hobbies and lifestyle.

Diverse Selection:

Offer a variety of items in different price ranges to accommodate the budgets of all your guests. Include both practical and sentimental items.

Online and In-Store:

Many retailers offer online registries, making shopping easy for guests. Some couples also register in-store, where they can scan items, they love.

Communicate:

Share your registry information on your wedding website, save-the-date cards, or wedding invitations. Be polite when sharing your registry, emphasizing that gifts are entirely optional.

2. Gift Etiquette:

Gifts are tokens of love; gift etiquette is a way to express gratitude.

Understanding gift etiquette is essential in ensuring your wedding gifts are received and managed gracefully. Follow these guidelines:

Receiving Gifts:

As you receive gifts, have a designated area to store them. Create a system to track who gave what to facilitate the thank-you card process.

Thank-You Cards:

1. Send thank-you cards to express your gratitude.

2. Personalize each card by mentioning the specific gift and how much it means.

3. Send them out within a few months of the wedding.

Gift Registries:

While it's perfectly acceptable to have a registry, it's not polite to include registry information on your wedding invitations. Share it through your wedding website or by word of mouth.

Cash Gifts:

For guests who opt to give cash gifts, thank them for their generosity in your thank-you cards. You can use cash gifts for various purposes, such as your honeymoon or savings.

Handling Duplicate Gifts:

It's not uncommon to receive duplicate gifts. In such cases, thank the giver for their thoughtfulness and consider returning or exchanging the extra item.

3. Thank-You Cards:

Thank-you cards are the bridge between you and your guests, expressing your appreciation.

Thank-you cards are an essential part of the wedding gift process. Here's how to handle them gracefully:

Timeliness:

Send thank-you cards within two to three months of your wedding. Aim to complete them sooner rather than later.

Personal Touch:

Make each thank-you card personal by mentioning the specific gift and how you plan to use it. Express your appreciation genuinely.

Photographs:

Consider including a photograph from your wedding day in the thank-you card to add a personal touch.

Helpers and Contributors:

Remember to send thank-you cards to anyone who contributed to your wedding, such as vendors, parents, and those who helped with planning.

Online or Handwritten:

While handwritten cards are more traditional, online tools can help streamline the process if you have many to send. However, a handwritten note adds a personal touch.

Your wedding registry, gift etiquette, and thank-you cards are all part of the journey toward creating a memorable and gracious wedding experience. By building your registry thoughtfully, understanding gift etiquette, and sending heartfelt thank-you cards, you'll express your appreciation to your loved ones and create a lasting connection between your wedding day and the love you share.

CHAPTER 7

Catering and Cake Selection:

Catering and the wedding cake are not just elements of sustenance; they're a feast for the senses and an expression of your love. From crafting a menu that tantalizes taste buds to selecting the ideal beverages and a wedding cake that leaves a sweet impression, this book guides you through the delectable journey of catering and cake selection for your wedding.

1. Menu Planning:

Your wedding menu is an edible love story, reflecting your tastes as a couple

Menu planning is an exciting part of wedding preparation. To ensure your guests have a memorable culinary experience, follow these steps:

Consider Dietary Preferences:

Be mindful of your guests' dietary preferences and restrictions. Include options for vegetarians, vegans, and those with food allergies.

Cuisine and Style:

Choose a cuisine that reflects your tastes and aligns with your wedding theme. You could opt for a formal sit-down meal, a buffet, or a casual food truck style.

Tastings:

Schedule tastings with potential caterers. Sample the menu items to ensure they meet your expectations in terms of flavor and presentation.

Customization:

Collaborate with the caterer to customize the menu. Incorporate items that hold personal significance or represent your cultural background.

Hors d'oeuvres and Appetizers:

Remember hors d'oeuvres and appetizers to keep guests satisfied during cocktail hour. These can be an opportunity to showcase your favorite flavors and ingredients.

2. Beverage Selection

Beverages enhance the dining experience and are a toast to your future.

Beverage selection is just as important as the food. Here's how to curate the perfect drink options:

Alcoholic and non-alcoholic:

Offer a selection of alcoholic and non-alcoholic beverages to cater to all your guests. Include options such as wine, beer, and signature cocktails.

Signature Drinks:

Create signature cocktails that reflect your personality or are named after meaningful places or experiences in your relationship.

Toast Options:

Choose a special champagne or sparkling wine for toast. Be sure to have non-alcoholic options for those who don't drink alcohol.

Beverage Stations:

Consider having beverage stations, such as a coffee bar or a water station with infused water, for guests to enjoy throughout the event.

Glassware and Presentation:

Pay attention to glassware and presentation. The way beverages are served can enhance the overall dining experience.

3. Wedding Cake and Desserts:

Your wedding cake is a centerpiece, and desserts are sweet memories in the making.

The wedding cake and desserts are an indulgent and visually stunning aspect of your celebration. Here's how to navigate these delectable choices:

Cake Design:

Choose a cake design that aligns with your wedding theme and decor. Consider options like traditional tiered cakes, naked cakes, or themed cakes.

Flavor Selection:

Select cake flavors that resonate with your tastes. Common choices include vanilla, chocolate, red velvet, and lemon. Opt for multiple cake flavors if you have multiple tiers.

Dessert Table:

Create a dessert table with a variety of sweet treats like cupcakes, macarons, and mini pastries; this allows your guests to indulge in a variety of flavors.

Cake Topper:

Personalize your cake with a unique cake topper that reflects your personality or the theme of your wedding.

Cake-Cutting Ceremony:

Make the cake-cutting ceremony a memorable moment. Discuss the details with your photographer to capture it beautifully.

Catering and cake selection for your wedding is an opportunity to express your culinary preferences and create a delightful experience for your guests. By thoughtfully planning your menu, selecting beverages that suit all tastes, and choosing a wedding cake and desserts that make a sweet impression, you ensure that your wedding day is a feast for the senses and an expression of your love as a couple. These decisions go beyond satisfying hunger; they create lasting memories of your special day.

CHAPTER 8

Entertainment and Music:

Entertainment and music are the heartbeats of your wedding celebration. They set the mood, create unforgettable moments, and keep the dance floor alive. From choosing between live musicians and DJs to crafting the perfect playlist and considering unique entertainment ideas, this book will guide you through the delightful world of wedding entertainment and music.

1. Hiring Musicians or DJs:

Live musicians and DJs bring their unique styles to your special day.

The choice between live musicians and DJs is an essential decision that shapes the musical experience of your wedding. **Here's how to make the proper selection:**

Live Musicians:

Musical Styles:

Select live musicians based on the style of music you prefer. Options range from classical string quartets to acoustic guitarists, vocalists, or even a full band.

Atmosphere:

Live musicians add an authentic and elegant touch to your wedding. They can create a romantic, intimate atmosphere for your ceremony or cocktail hour.

Repertoire:

Discuss your favorite songs with the musicians. Many live performers can learn and perform specific songs to personalize their wedding music.

DJs:

Versatility:

DJs offer various music genres, making catering to diverse tastes easy and keeping the dance floor lively.

Song Selection:

Work with your DJ to curate a playlist with your favorite songs and music that will appeal to your guests.

MC Services:

DJs can also serve as your Master of Ceremonies, guiding the reception and making important announcements.

2. Creating the Perfect Playlist:

Your playlist is a love story in notes and lyrics. Crafting the perfect playlist is all about personalization and creating an emotional connection with your guests. Here's how to do it:

Your Love Story:

Include songs that hold sentimental value, such as the song you first danced to or tracks that have been significant during your relationship.

Guest Involvement:

Consider incorporating song requests from your guests. You can include request cards with your invitations or create a dedicated section on your wedding website.

Variety:

Create a playlist with a mix of musical styles and tempos to cater to all age groups and musical tastes.

Transition and Flow:

Work with your DJ or musicians to ensure smooth transitions between songs and musical sets; this keeps the dance floor energy high.

3. Entertainment Ideas:

Beyond music, consider unique entertainment ideas that will leave a lasting impression.

Incorporating unique entertainment ideas can elevate your wedding experience.

Here are some creative suggestions:

Photo Booths:

Set up a photo booth with props, allowing guests to capture fun and memorable moments.

Live Performances:

Hire dancers, magicians, or other live performers to entertain your guests during the reception.

Interactive Games:

Create interactive games or activities that engage your guests, such as trivia, lawn games, or a karaoke competition.

Surprises:

Plan a surprise performance or activity guests won't expect, such as a flash mob dance or a fireworks display.

Cultural Elements:

If your wedding celebrates a particular culture, consider incorporating cultural entertainment, like traditional dances or music.

Entertainment and music are key ingredients in making your wedding a memorable celebration. Whether you choose live musicians or a DJ, craft a playlist that tells your love story, and consider unique entertainment ideas. You'll create an unforgettable experience for you and your guests. These decisions go beyond the technical aspects of sound and lights; they're about making your wedding day a vibrant, joyful celebration of your love.

CHAPTER 9

Flowers and Décor:

Flowers and decor are pivotal in transforming your wedding into a visual masterpiece. From elegant floral arrangements and bridal bouquets to ceremony decor and reception centerpieces, this book will guide you through the enchanting world of wedding flowers and decor.

1. Floral Arrangements and Bouquets:

Floral arrangements are the heart of your wedding's aesthetic.

The proper floral arrangements and bouquets can set the tone for your wedding day.

Here's how to make the most of these enchanting blooms:

Color Palette:

Select a color palette that complements your wedding's theme and style. Coordinate your floral choices with your chosen colors.

Bridal Bouquet:

Your bridal bouquet is your most important accessory. Select blooms that speak to your personality and style and blend harmoniously with your wedding gown.

Bridesmaid Bouquets:

The bouquets carried by your bridesmaids should echo your chosen color palette and style while still being unique.

Centerpieces:

Choose centerpieces that reflect the mood and ambience of your wedding reception. Consider a mix of high and low centerpieces for variety.

Corsages and Boutonnieres:

Remember corsages for mothers and grandmothers and boutonnieres for fathers and grandfathers. These small details complete the overall floral scheme.

Floral Trends:

Stay updated on the latest floral trends to incorporate modern or seasonal elements into your arrangements.

2. Ceremony Décor:

Decor at your ceremony creates a stunning backdrop for your vows.

Your ceremony is the most pivotal part of your wedding day, and the decor sets the stage for this meaningful moment. Consider the following tips:

Altar Decor:

Whether it's a traditional arch, a rustic wooden backdrop, or a natural setting, choose decor that aligns with your theme and complements your color palette.

Aisle Decor:

Use floral arrangements, lanterns, or hanging flowers to add beauty and style to the aisle; this is where your grand entrance happens, so make it unique.

Seating:

Select seating arrangements that enhance the decor. You can use chair covers, sashes, or floral accents to create a cohesive look.

Lighting:

Consider how lighting can accentuate the décor. Candles, string lights, or lanterns can create a romantic ambience.

Personal Touches:

Add personal touches to your ceremony decors, such as framed photos, love quotes, or mementoes that tell your unique love story.

3. Reception Centerpieces:

Reception centerpieces are the focal point of your wedding celebration.

The reception is where your guests will spend most of their time celebrating, making the centerpieces an essential element of your decor.

Here's how to make them exceptional:

Table Styles:

Consider different table styles, from round to long banquet tables, and choose centerpieces that suit the layout.

Floral Variety:

A mix of flower varieties adds depth and texture to your centerpieces. Incorporate your chosen color palette.

Vases and Containers:

Explore a variety of vases, containers, and candleholders to achieve different looks. Consider vintage finds or unique containers that hold personal meaning.

Height Variation:

Use a mix of high and low centerpieces to create visual interest and accommodate guest conversation.

Table Linens:

The choice of table linens can complement or contrast with your centerpieces. It's all about creating a cohesive look.

Favors:

Some couples incorporate wedding favors into their centerpieces as a thoughtful gesture to guests. Flowers and decor are more than just aesthetics; they are the artistic expression of your love story. You'll transform your wedding day into a visual masterpiece remembered for its beauty and elegance by carefully selecting your floral arrangements, ceremony decor, and reception centerpieces.

These elements go beyond ornamentation; they reflect your unique love, your shared vision, and the celebration of your future together.

Chapter 10
Photography and Videography:

Photography and videography are the cherished time capsules of your wedding day. They capture the essence of your love story, the candid moments, and the emotions that make the day unforgettable. From choosing the right wedding photographer to ensuring you capture every moment and considering the art of videography and cinematography, this book will guide you through the beautiful world of wedding photography and videography.

1. Choosing Your Wedding Photographer:

Your wedding photographer is the storyteller who crafts your love story in images.

Choosing the right wedding photographer is crucial, as these images will be a lasting reminder of your special day. Here's how to make the best choice:

Style and Aesthetics:

Explore different photography styles, such as traditional, photojournalistic, or fine art. Choose a style that resonates with your vision and preferences.

Portfolio and Experience:

Review the portfolios of potential photographers. Look for a variety of wedding shots that showcase their skills and experience.

Personality Fit:

Your photographer will be with you during intimate moments, so having a good rapport is essential. Ensure your personalities mesh well.

Interviews and References:

Schedule interviews with your shortlisted photographers. Ask for references from past clients to get insights into their professionalism and work ethic.

Packages and Pricing:

Discuss packages, pricing, and any additional services with your chosen photographer. Make sure there are no hidden costs.

2. Capturing the Moments:

Capturing moments goes beyond staged poses; it's about preserving the emotions.

The magic of wedding photography lies in the moments captured, so work with your photographer to ensure every significant moment is preserved:

Getting Ready:

Document the anticipation and excitement as you and your partner prepare for the day.

Ceremony:

Capture the heartfelt exchange of vows, the ring exchange, and the first kiss.

Candid Moments:

Ask your photographer to focus on candid shots that capture genuine emotions, from laughter to tears.

Family and Group Photos:

Remember to include formal group shots, including family, bridal party, and friends.

Details:

Document the intricate details, such as your dress, bouquet, and venue decor.

Reception:

Capture the joy of the first dance, toasts, and all the celebratory moments.

3. Videography and Cinematography:

Videography captures the moving moments, the emotions, and the sounds of your day.

Videography adds another dimension to your wedding memories by preserving your special day's moving images and sounds. Here's how to make the most of this art:

Choosing a Videographer:

Much like selecting a photographer, choose a videographer whose style aligns with your vision. Review their previous work to get a sense of their skills and storytelling.

Highlight Reel:

Work with your videographer to create a highlight reel that captures the essence of your day in a short, cinematic format.

Ceremony and Reception:

Ensure that the crucial moments of your ceremony and reception are recorded fully, allowing you to relive them.

Sound and music:

Pay attention to audio quality. Ensure that vows and speeches are captured clearly. Consider incorporating music that holds meaning to you both.

Drone Footage:

Some videographers offer drone footage for unique aerial perspectives of your wedding venue and surroundings.

Editing:

Discuss the editing process with your videographer. Ask for revisions and customization options for the final video.

Wedding photography and videography are the visual storytellers of your love story. By choosing the right photographer, capturing the moments that matter, and considering the art of videography and cinematography, you ensure that your wedding day is preserved in a way that evokes emotions and memories for years to come. These decisions go beyond technical details; they're about crafting a visual narrative of your love, the moments, and the celebration that defines your wedding.

CHAPTER 11
Planning the Perfect Honeymoon:

Your honeymoon is the beginning of your lifelong adventure, a time to celebrate your love and create cherished memories. From choosing the ideal destination to making travel arrangements and mastering the art of packing, this book is your guide to planning the perfect honeymoon after your wedding.

1. Destination Ideas:

Selecting the perfect destination is the first step toward a dreamy honeymoon.

Choosing the right destination sets the tone for your honeymoon.

Here's how to decide on the perfect spot:

Honeymoon Style:

Consider the type of experience you desire. Are you looking for relaxation on a sandy beach, adventure in the mountains, or cultural exploration in a city?

Travel Preferences:

Think about the travel distance and time you're comfortable with. Would you prefer a short domestic trip or an international adventure?

Budget:

Establish a honeymoon budget and select a destination that fits your financial plan. Some destinations are more cost-effective than others.

Season and Weather:

Check potential destinations' climate and weather conditions, particularly if you have a particular season in mind.

Honeymoon Packages:

Explore honeymoon packages offered by resorts and travel agencies. These often include special perks for newlyweds.

2. Travel Arrangements:

Efficient travel arrangements pave the way for a stress-free honeymoon.

Once you've chosen your destination, it's time to make travel arrangements.

Here's how to ensure a smooth journey:

Booking Flights and Accommodations:

Book your flights and accommodations early to secure the best prices and availability.

Travel Insurance:

Consider purchasing travel insurance to protect against unexpected events, such as trip cancellations or medical emergencies.

Itinerary Planning:

Create a detailed itinerary that includes flight information, hotel reservations, transportation details, and activity bookings.

Passport and Visa:

Check the passport and visa requirements for your destination. Ensure your documents are up-to-date well before your trip.

Travel Wallet:

Organize your travel documents in a secure wallet or organizer, including passports, visas, and reservation confirmations.

Health Preparations:

If travelling internationally, consult your doctor about any vaccinations or health precautions you should take for your destination.

3. Packing Tips:

Efficient packing ensures you have everything you need without unnecessary clutter.

Packing for your honeymoon is an art, as it's essential to strike the right balance between having everything you need and avoiding overpacking.

Clothing:

Pack a mix of clothing suitable for your destination and planned activities. Remember essentials like swimwear, comfortable walking shoes, and formal attire if needed.

Travel Essentials:

Include essential travel items like your passport, tickets, travel adapters, and chargers. Remember to use your camera to capture memories.

Toiletries:

Pack travel-sized toiletries to save space and avoid spills. Consider necessities like sunscreen, bug spray, and any specific skincare products.

Medications:

If you take prescription medications, ensure an adequate supply for your trip.

Travel Accessories:

Consider practical accessories like a neck pillow, eye mask, or noise-cancelling headphones to enhance your comfort during the journey.

Honeymoon Essentials:

Bring any items specific to your honeymoon, such as special lingerie, romantic gifts, or wedding-related memorabilia.

Pack Smart:

Use packing cubes or luggage organizers to keep your suitcase neat and organized. Roll your clothes to save space and reduce wrinkles.

Planning the perfect honeymoon is a delightful part of your wedding journey. By carefully selecting the ideal destination, making efficient travel arrangements, and mastering the art of packing, you ensure that your post-wedding adventure is a beautiful beginning to your life together. These decisions go beyond logistics; they're about creating cherished memories and savoring the love that binds you as a couple.

CHAPTER 12:

Final Preparations:

The days leading up to your wedding are a whirlwind of excitement, anticipation, and last-minute preparations. As you approach your special day, the final touches are essential to ensure everything runs smoothly. This book explores the critical aspects of preparing for your wedding, including the wedding rehearsal, creating a day-of timeline, and handling those inevitable last-minute details.

1. The Wedding Rehearsal:

The wedding rehearsal is a practice run for your special day.

A wedding rehearsal allows you, your bridal party, and family members to get comfortable with the ceremony's order and logistics.

Here's how to make the most of it:

Schedule and Venue:

Set a date and time for the rehearsal, usually the day before the wedding. Conduct it at your ceremony venue or a nearby location.

Participants:

Ensure that everyone involved in the ceremony, from the officiant to the flower girl, is present. It's a time to clarify roles and responsibilities.

Walk-Through:

Practice walking down the aisle, exchanging vows, and any special rituals or customs you plan to include in the ceremony.

Ceremony Details:

Discuss the specific elements of the ceremony, such as the processional order, music cues, and readings; this is also the time to go over any special instructions for participants.

Timing:

Use the rehearsal to establish the timing of the ceremony. Consider factors like the length of the processional and the exchange of rings.

2. Day-Of-Timeline:

Creating a day-of timeline ensures that your wedding day runs smoothly.

A well-structured day-to-day timeline is crucial for keeping your wedding day organized and stress-free. **Here's how to create one:**

Start Early:

Begin with the start time of the ceremony and work backwards. Include every step, from hair and makeup to the last dance.

Be Realistic:

Give yourself extra time for each task to account for potential delays. It's better to have a buffer for unexpected situations.

Assign Duties:

Designate someone, such as a wedding coordinator or a trusted friend, to oversee the timeline and ensure everything is on track.

Photographer/Videographer:

Coordinate with your photographer and videographer to ensure they capture all the crucial moments per the timeline.

Include Downtime:

Remember to schedule breaks and time for you and your partner to relax and savor the day.

3. Handling Last-Minute Details:

Last-minute details are an essential part of wedding preparation.
Several last-minute details require your attention in the final days before your wedding.
Here's how to manage them:

Final Confirmations:
Contact all your vendors to confirm arrangements, from the caterer and florist to the photographer and musicians.

Emergency Kit:

Create an emergency kit with safety pins, stain remover, tissues, and necessary medications.

Payment Envelopes:

Prepare an envelope with final payments and tips for vendors and distribute it by a trusted person on your wedding day.

Apparel and Accessories:

Ensure your wedding attire, shoes, and accessories are clean, pressed, and ready for the big day.

Marriage License:

Remember to pick up your marriage license if you still need to do so.

Communication:

Share the day-of timeline with your bridal party and key family members. Make sure everyone knows their responsibilities.

The final preparations for your wedding are about ensuring everything is in place and running smoothly for your special day. By conducting a wedding rehearsal, creating a day-of timeline, and handling those last-minute details, you'll ensure that your wedding day unfolds seamlessly, allowing you to focus on celebrating your love and the joy of the moment. These details are not just logistics; they are the final strokes on a canvas of memories that will last a lifetime.

CHAPTER 13

The Big Day:

Your wedding day, the culmination of your love story, celebrates your commitment to each other. As you step into the grandeur of this moment, getting ready, the ceremony and the reception are the day's highlights. In this book, we'll explore the magic of your wedding day, from those final moments of preparation to the exchange of vows and the following joyful celebration.

1. Getting Ready:

The getting-ready phase sets the tone for your special day.

The process of getting ready is about more than preparing physically.

It's about embracing the emotions and anticipating the day.

Here's how to make this time unforgettable:

Hair and makeup:

Trust your chosen hair and makeup artists to enhance your natural beauty, ensuring you look and feel radiant.

Getting Dressed:

Slip into your wedding attire with the help of your bridesmaids or family members. These moments of dressing are a cherished part of your wedding day.

Photography:

Have your photographer capture candid shots of you and your bridal party as you prepare.

These images hold memories of laughter, excitement, and anticipation.

Gift Exchange:

Many couples exchange gifts or handwritten letters during this time, adding a personal touch to the day.

Reflection:

Take a moment for yourself to reflect on the significance of the day. Breathe, calm your nerves, and prepare to walk down the aisle.

2. The Ceremony:

The ceremony is the heart of your wedding day, where you make lifelong promises.

The wedding ceremony is the emotional core of your day.

Here's how to make it a memorable experience:

Processional:

The processional marks the beginning of your ceremony. As you and your bridal party walk down the aisle, all eyes are on you.

Vows and Exchange of Rings:

The exchange of vows and rings is the centerpiece of the ceremony. These are the promises that bind you together for life.

Unity Rituals:

If you've chosen to include unity rituals like candle lighting or sand ceremonies, they can add depth and meaning to your ceremony.

Readings and Music:

Incorporate readings or musical performances that hold significance for your relationship. They add a personal touch to the ceremony.

Officiant:

Your officiant guides the ceremony and plays a vital role in creating a heartfelt atmosphere.

Pronouncement:

When you're pronounced as a married couple, embrace the applause and the joy of the moment.

3. The Reception:

The reception is a time for joy, celebration, and togetherness.

The reception is a celebration of your love and commitment.

Here's how to create a memorable reception:

Entrance:

Make a grand entrance as a married couple, with cheers and applause from your guests.

First Dance:

Share your first dance as a married couple—a moment that's both intimate and a highlight of the evening.

Toasts:

Let your loved ones make toast, sharing their well wishes and heartfelt sentiments.

Dinner and dancing:

The reception dinner is a time for indulgence, followed by dancing and celebration. Choose a meal that delights your guests and create a dance floor that keeps everyone moving.

Cutting the Cake:

Cutting the wedding cake is a sweet tradition. Remember to capture this moment for your album.

Favors and Keepsakes:

Consider offering wedding favors or keepsakes to thank your guests for being part of your celebration.

Your wedding day, the culmination of your love story, is a joyful and emotional journey. You'll ensure that your special day reflects your love and commitment by embracing the getting ready process, cherishing the ceremony, and creating a memorable reception. These moments are not just formalities; they are the story chapters celebrating your unique passion, shared promises, and the joy that binds you as a couple.

Chapter 14:

Post-Wedding Bliss

As the last note of your wedding celebration fades away, a new chapter of your journey begins. Post-wedding life is not just about settling into everyday routines; it's about preserving the memories of your special day, showing gratitude to your loved ones, and gracefully transitioning into life as a married couple. This book explores how to embrace post-wedding bliss and make the most of this exciting new chapter.

1. Preserving Memories:

Preserving the memories of your wedding day keeps the magic alive.

Your wedding day was a whirlwind of emotions, and you want to ensure those cherished moments are never forgotten.

Here's how to preserve the memories:

Photo Albums:

Create a beautiful photo album with your favorite images from your wedding. It's a tangible keepsake that you can revisit whenever you wish.

Videos:

If you hired a videographer, relive the day by watching your wedding video. It captures the sights, sounds, and emotions of the day.

Frame Your Memories:

Select a few of your favorite photos to frame and display in your home. This way, you can admire them daily.

Keepsakes:

Keep small items like your wedding program, vows, or a bouquet piece in a memory box. Add to it over the years.

Anniversary Traditions:

Consider starting anniversary traditions, like watching your wedding video or revisiting your venue.

2. Thanking Your Guests:

Expressing gratitude is a beautiful way to extend the joy of your wedding.

Your wedding day was made even more special by the presence and support of your friends and family. Express your appreciation by thanking your guests.

Thank-You Cards:

Send personalized thank-you cards to everyone who attended your wedding. Mention the gift they gave and express your gratitude for their presence.

Gifts:

For members of your bridal party and immediate family, consider giving them small, thoughtful gifts as tokens of appreciation.

Online Photo Albums:

Share your wedding photos in an online album or on social media. This way, your guests can relive the day and feel part of your continued journey.

Post-Wedding Celebration:

Host a casual post-wedding gathering or a dinner to show appreciation and relive the day's joy with your guests.

3. Navigating life as a Married Couple:

Life after the wedding is a journey of love and growth.

As a married couple, life holds new adventures and opportunities for growth.

Here's how to navigate this journey together:

Set Goals:

Discuss your long-term goals and dreams as a couple. Whether buying a home, travelling the world, or starting a family, having shared objectives strengthens your bond.

Communication:

Open, honest communication is vital to a healthy marriage. Be sure to express your feelings, needs, and concerns to one another.

Quality Time:

Continue to prioritize quality time together. Date nights and memorable moments are essential to maintaining the connection you built during your courtship.

Compromise:

Marriage often involves compromise. Finding solutions that work for both of you and respecting each other's individuality is essential.

Adventures and Traditions:

Embrace new adventures together, and create the traditions and routines that make your marriage unique.

Post-wedding life is a journey of love, growth, and shared experiences.

By preserving the memories of your special day, expressing gratitude to your loved ones, and gracefully navigating life as a married couple, you'll create a strong foundation for your lifelong commitment. These moments go beyond the wedding day; they are the ongoing chapters in the beautiful story of your marriage.

Conclusion:

In closing, "The Ultimate Guide to Perfect Weddings" has been your dedicated companion on a remarkable journey – your journey to the perfect wedding. As you close the final chapter and begin to embark on your own unique wedding planning adventure, remember that this is a story of love, commitment, and dreams fulfilled.

Your perfect wedding journey begins now and is a path as individual as your love story. While this guide has provided you with the knowledge and inspiration to navigate the intricate details of planning a flawless wedding, it's essential to remember that your wedding is a reflection of your love and love alone.

Your journey is a time to create memories, share moments, and make lasting promises. It's a time to honor traditions, break new ground, and define your rules. The journey is filled with excitement, anticipation, and, yes, a few challenges along the way, but these moments are all part of the adventure.

Whether planning a grand celebration or an intimate gathering, your wedding is a testament to your love and commitment to a future filled with shared dreams and cherished memories. It's a day when two souls unite, and a new chapter begins.

So, as you embark on your perfect wedding journey, take a deep breath, smile, and remember that love is at the heart of it all. Embrace the ups and downs, savor the moments, and cherish every step of the way. Your perfect wedding is a celebration of love, a journey of a lifetime, and it begins now. I am wishing you a beautiful and love-filled wedding day.